The Balm Of Gilead: Or The Recovery Of Man's Fall By Redemption

Thomas H. Holmes

THE

BALM OF GILEAD;

OR, THE

Recovery of Man's Fall

BY REDEMPTION.

Being a short and concise account of Man's happiness in the Garden of Eden, his disobedience and Fall, and Expulsion from Paradise, and his glorious Redemption by Jesus Christ the true Messiah.

BY THOMAS H. HOLMES,

AUTHOR

Of the " New Year's Gift," "A Visit to Buxton," &c., &c., &c.

" Is there no balm in Gilead; is there no physician there? Why then is not the health of my people recovered."
Jer. viii. 22.
" And the leaves of the tree were for the healing of the nations."
Rev. xxii 2.

LONDON:
LONGMAN & CO., PATERNOSTER ROW;
J. W. ADAM, LIBRARY, MATLOCK; W. & W. PIKE, DERBY; AND J. GOODWIN, BAKEWELL.
1847.

TO THE

REV. H. C. SMITH,

INCUMBENT OF MONYASH,

THIS LITTLE WORK IS

BY THE AUTHOR MOST RESPECTFULLY,

AND GRATEFULLY DEDICATED,

WITH THE CONVICTION

THAT

A NAME SO EMINENTLY AND SO JUSTLY

DISTINGUISHED FOR LEARNING, RELIGION,

AND PIETY WILL PRESERVE

HIS HUMBLE EFFORTS FROM

OBLIVION.

PREFACE.

IT will be to little purpose, the Author presumes, to offer any reasons, why this little work appears in public, for it is ten to one whether he gives the true, and if he does, it is much greater odds, whether the gentle reader is so courteous as to believe him. He could tell the world, according to the laudable custom of Prefaces, that it was through the irresistible importunity of friends, or some other excuse of ancient renown, that he ventured it to the press: but he thought it much better to leave every man to judge for himself, and then

he would be sure to satisfy himself; for,
let what will be pretended, people are
grown so very apt to fancy they are always
in the right, that, unless it hit their humour, it is immediately condemned for a
sham and hypocrisy.

In short, that which wants an excuse
for being in print, ought not to have been
printed at all."* But whether the ensuing
little work deserves to stand in that class
the world must have leave to determine.
And what faults the true judgment of the
Gentleman may find out, it is to be hoped
his candour and good humour will easily
pardon.

But to please every one would be a new
thing; and to write so as to please nobody
would be as new; for even the most irreli-
gious and abominable writers have their
admirers.

* Rev. John Pomfret.

The Author is not so fond of fame to desire it from the injudicious many; nor of so mortified a temper not to wish it from the discerning few, for it is not the multitude of applauses, but the good sense of the applauders, which establishes a valuable reputation; and if a Christian or a sinner say it is well he will not be at all solicitous how great the majority may be to the contrary.

T. H. H.

Lime Tree Cottage,
Matlock,
Anno, 1847.

THE

𝔖acreð Name 𝔍esus.

~~~~~~~~~~~~

Jehovah: God: Almighty: Jah: I am:
Emanuel: Shiloh: Lord of Hosts: the Lamb:
Secret Desire of Nations: Bridegroom: Lord:
Unchangeable: Eternal: King: the Word:
Saviour: the Branch: the Lord: our Rigteousness:
Counsellor: Root of Jesse: Prince of Peace:
Holy: True: Faithful: Brother: Father: Friend:
Redeemer: High Priest: Life: Beginning: End:
Immortal: Shepherd: Husband: Shield and Son:
Seed of the Woman: precious Corner Stone:
The Way: the Truth: Messiah: God alone.

Introductory Chapter.

PROPHECY.

And I will put enmity between thee and the woman, and between thy seed and her seed ; it shall bruise thy head ; and thou shalt bruise his heel. Gen. iii. 15.

And in thee shall all families of the earth be blessed. Gen. xii. 3.

Kiss the Son, lest he be angry and ye perish from the way, when his wrath is kindled but a little. Blessed are all they that put their trust in him. Ps. i. ii. 18.

The Lord hath sworn, and will not repent, Thou art a priest for ever, after the order of Melchizedek. Ps. cx. 4.

The people that walked in darkness have seen a great light : they that dwell in the land of the shadow of death, upon them hath the light shined. Isa. ix. 2.

For unto us a child is born, unto us a son is given: and the government shall be upon his shoulder: and his name shall be called Wonderful, Counsellor, The mighty God, The Everlasting Father, The Prince of Peace. Ibib. ix. 6. And in that day there shall be a root of Jesse, which shall stand for an ensign of the people; to it shall the Gentiles seek; and his rest shall be glorious. Ibib. xi. 10.

The wilderness and the solitary place shall be glad for them: and the desert shall rejoice, and blossom as the rose. Ibib. xxxv. 1.

Then the eyes of the blind shall be opened, and the ears of the deaf shall be unstopped. Then shall the lame man leap as an hart, and the tongue of the dumb sing. Ibib. xxxv. 5, 6.

He shall feed his flock like a shepherd, he shall gather the lambs with his arms, and carry them in his bosom, and shall gently lead those that are with young. Ibib. xl. 11.

But he was wounded for our transgressions, he was bruised for our iniquities: the chastisement of our peace was upon him, and with his stripes we are healed. Ibib. liii. 5.

The Spirit of the Lord God is upon me because the Lord hath anointed me to preach good tidings unto the meek; he hath sent me to bind up the broken-hearted, to proclaim liberty to the captives, and the opening of the prison to them that are bound. Ibib. lxi. 1.

Behold, the days come saith the Lord that I will raise unto David a righteous Branch. And this is the name whereby he shall be called, THE LORD OUR RIGHTEOUSNESS. Jer. xxiii. 5, 6.

And they all shall have one Shepherd. Ez. xxvii. 24.

But thou Bethlehem Ephratah, though thou be little among the thousands of Judah, yet out of thee shall he come forth unto me, that is to be ruler in Israel: whose

goings forth have been from of old, from
everlasting.   Micah v. 2.

Rejoice greatly, O daughter of Zion ;
shout, O daughter of Jerusalem : behold
thy King cometh unto thee : he is just and
having salvation : lowly, and riding upon
an ass, and upon a colt the foal of an ass.
Zech. ix. 9.

Awake, O sword, against my shepherd,
and against the man that is my fellow,
saith the Lord of hosts : smite the shepherd, and the sheep shall be scattered.
Zech. xiii. 7.

Because thou wilt not leave my soul in
hell, neither wilt thou suffer thine Holy
One to see corruption.

Fulfilment.

I bring you good tidings of great joy,
which shall be to all people. For unto you
is born this day, in the city of David, a
Saviour, which is Christ the Lord. Luke
ii. 10, 11.

Now is the judgment of this world: now shall the prince of this world be cast out, St. John xii. 31.

Blessed be the Lord God of Israel: for he hath visited and redeemed his people. And hath raised up an horn of salvation for us in the house of his servant David. To perform the mercy promised to our fathers, and to remember his holy covenant. The oath which he sware to our father Abraham. Luke i. 68, 69, 72, 73.

And, behold, a voice out of the cloud, which said, This is my beloved Son in whom I am well pleased: hear ye Him. Matt. xvii, 5.

And being made perfect, he became the author of eternal salvation unto all them that obey him. Called of God an High Priest, after the order of Melchizedek. Heb. v. 9, 10.

I am come a light into the world, that whosoever believeth on me should not abide in darkness. St. John xii. 46.

And he called his name Jesus. Matt.
i. 25.

Wherefore God hath highly exalted him,
and given him a name which is above every
name: that at the name of Jesus every knee
shall bow, of things in heaven and things
on earth. Phil. ii. 9, 10.

Come unto me all ye that labour and are
heavy laden, and I will give you rest.
Take my yoke upon you and learn of me,
for I am meek and lowly in heart, and ye
shall find rest unto your souls; For my
yoke is easy, and my burden is light.
Matt. xi. 28—30.

And in the same hour he cured many of
their infirmities and plagues, and of evil
spirits, and unto many that were blind he
gave sight. Then Jesus answering, said,
unto them, Go your way and tell John
what things ye have seen and heard; how
that the blind see, the lame walk, the
lepers are cleansed, the deaf hear, the dead

are raised, to the poor the Gospel is preached. Luke vii. 21, 22.

I am the good shepherd, and know my
sheep, and am known of mine. And I
give unto them eternal life, and they shall
never perish, neither shall any man pluck
them out of my hand. St. John x. 14—28.

Then did they spit in his face, and buf-
feted him, and others smote him with the
palms of their hands. Matt. xxvi. 6, 7.

And they crucified him. Matt. xxvii. 35.

But God raised him from the dead.
Acts xiii. 30.

Though he were a Son, yet learned he
obedience by the things which he suffered:
And being made perfect, he became the
author of eternal salvation unto all them
that obey him. Heb. v. 8, 9. Also see
1st of Peter ii. 21—25.

And the eyes of all them that were in
the synagogue were fastened on him. And
he began to say unto them, This day is this

Scripture fulfilled in your ears. Luke iv.
20, 21.

I have found David, the son of Jesse, a
man after mine own heart, which shall
fulfil all my will.—Of this man's seed hath
God, according to his promise, raised unto
Israel a Saviour, Jesus. Acts xiii. 22, 23.

For ye were as sheep going astray, but
are now returned unto the Shepherd and
Bishop of your souls. 1 Pet. ii. 25.

The shepherds said one to another, let
us now go even to Bethlehem, and see this
thing which is come to pass, which the
Lord hath made known unto us. And they
came with haste, and found Mary and
Joseph, and the Babe lying in a manger.
Luke ii. 15, 16

And they brought the colt to Jesus, and
cast their garments on him : and he sat
upon him. And they that went before,
and they that followed, cried, saying, Ho-
sanna : Blessed is he that cometh in the
name of the Lord. Mark xi. 7—9.

And Jesus saith unto them, all ye shall be offended, because of me this night : for it is written I will smite the Shepherd and the sheep shall be scattered. And they all forsook him and fled. St. Mark xiv. 27.

Fear not ye for I know that ye seek Jesus which was crucified. He is not here, for he is risen as he said. Come see the place where the Lord lay. Matt. xxviii. 5, 6.

He seeing this before, spake of the resurrection of Christ, that his soul was not left in hell, neither his flesh did see corruption. Acts ii. 31.

THE BALM OF GILEAD,

&c., &c.

CHAPTER I.

"Man fall's deceived,
Man therefore shall find grace."

"O unexampled love,
Love, no where to be found, less than divine!
Hail, Son of God, Saviour of men, thy name
Shall be the copious matter of my song.
Henceforth, and never shall my harp thy praise
Forget, nor from thy father's praise disjoin.
Milton, Par. Lost, Book 3.

"The seed of the woman shall bruise the serpent's head."

In the beginning the Lord Almighty made the heaven and the earth; and created all things therein; The first idea given of our habitual globe is that of a rude and

unintelligible chaos. For the earth was
without form, and void; and darkness was
upon the face of the great deep; but, by
the operation of the Spirit of God which
moved upon the face of the waters, this
confused mass was gradually separated,
harmonized, and wrought into this beautiful structure, with such exactness, and
variety of appearance, which from the ear-
liest ages to the present period, has filled
the breast of every pious individual with
sentiments of mingled gratitude, wonder,
and admiration.

After this stupendous work was accomplished, the Adorable Being, who in the
Old Testament is designated by the sacred
epithets God, Jehovah, and the great I am,
but who, in later ages, has revealed himself more fully in the person of his co-equal
and co-eternal son Jesus Christ, next commanded the light to shine out of darkness;
and by his eternal fiat, produced a glorious
day; for God said, Let there be light, and

there was light ; * and the light God called day ; and the darkness called he night ;
the next effect of creative power was to divide the waters from the waters.   The
firmament or lower heaven was expanded
to divide the upper from the lower waters,
the floods unanimously rushed into their
appointed bed and received the appellation
of seas ; and the dry land (now distinguished by the name of earth) was suddenly
covered with a verdant mantle, enriched
with innumerable trees and shrubs of every
variety, and embroidered with flowers of
every tint and fragrance.   The canopy of
heaven was, also, spangled with myriads
of stars ; and the sun and moon, those
greater luminaries, were so disposed as to
enlighten the newly created world, to divide the revolving seasons, and to form a
perpetual distinction between day and
night.

The waters were next replenished with

Gen. i. 3.

an abundant variety of fish, and a numerous host of other aquatic animals, which
inhabit the great deep; the birds of the
air, starting into existence, hailed with
mellifluous songs, their Maker's goodness;
and the teeming earth brought forth abun-
dantly her appropriate tribes.

Lastly, to complete his great design, and
eclipse the glory of all his preceding works,
God created man in his own image out of
the dust of the ground, and infused into
his nostrils the breath of immortality, in
consequence of which, Moses asserts that
"man became a living soul."

> For in his looks divine,
> The image of his glorious Maker did shine.

This favorite of the Deity was immediately invested with unlimited power and
authority over every other created being;
and all beasts of the field, and birds of the
air, fishes in the sea, and every living
thing that creepeth upon the earth, was

brought unto him to receive their respective names ; and for every living creature there was found a mate ; but for Adam there was not found a helpmate for him.* So the Lord, our Maker, in his everlasting mercy and goodness to mankind ; knowing it not condusive to man's happiness to reside alone ; formed a suitable companion for him, out of his own side, wherefore he gave her the appellation of woman, saying, " This is now bone of my bone, and flesh of my flesh ; she shall be called woman, because she was taken out of man. Therefore shall a man leave his father and his mother, and shall cleave unto his wife, and they shall be one flesh.*

Here, therefore, we have an excellent antidote against the blind superstitious and unscriptural fallacies of the Romish Church, who forbids her priests to marry ; for marriage is honourable in all, and the bed undefiled ; but whoremongers and adulterers, God will judge.†   But truly it appears

* Gen. ii. 20.   † Heb. xiii. 5.

they prefer the Pope's commands and laws sooner than God's; and seems to give assent to the words uttered by one of their learned divines, who blasphemously exclaimed, "We had better be without God's laws than the Pope's." And no doubt these are they which St. Paul said, should depart from the faith, giving heed to seducing spirits and doctrines of devils; speaking lies in hypocrisy; having their conscience seared with a hot iron. Forbidding to marry, and commanding to abstain from meats which God hath created to be received with thanksgiving of them which believe and know the truth.* But the time is not far distant, when that man of sin— who opposeth and exalteth himself above all that is called God, or that is worshipped, so that he as God sitteth in the temple of God, showing himself that he is God, shall be revealed; whom the Lord shall consume with the Spirit of his mouth, and shall destroy with the brightness of his coming.†

* Tim. iv. 1—3.　　† Thess. ii. 3, 4, 8.

CHAPTER II.

"To all delight of human sense exposed,
In narrow room, Nature's whole wealth, ye more,
A heav'n on earth: For blissful Paradise,
Of God the garden was, by him in th' east
Of Eden planted.   *   *   *
A happy rural seat of various view.
Groves whose rich trees wept odorous gums and
  balm ;
Others whose fruit burnished with golden rind,
Hung amiable   *   *   *
Flowers of all hue, and without thorn the rose.
Another side, umbrageous grots and caves,
Of cool recess o'er which the mantling vine
Lays forth her purple grape, and gently creeps
Luxuriant "———
                              Milton, Par. Lost.

When the Lord God had made Adam
and Eve, he planted a garden eastward in
Eden, and out of the ground he caused to
grow all manner of trees, which is pleasant
to the sight, and good for food, and in the
midst of the garden stood the tree of life.

  "High eminent, blooming embrosial fruit
  Of vegetable gold."

And next to the tree of life grew the tree
of knowledge of good and evil. In this
delightful garden he placed Adam and Eve
to dress it, and to keep it—not for the
purpose of servile labour, but for healthful
recreation and pleasure, and to preserve
them from a state of sloth and idleness,
which would be injurious both to their
health and happiness.

" For sloth consumes faster than labour wears."
Franklin.

And of all the fruit that grew upon all
the trees in the garden, they might freely
eat, only of the fruit that grew upon the
tree of the knowledge of good and evil they
were forbidden to eat, with this injunction,
—For in the day that thou eatest thereof
thou shalt surely die* Which they, no
doubt, thought an easy task.

" He who requires
From us no other service than to keep

Gen. ii. 17.

This one, this easy charge, of all the trees
In Paradise that bear delicious fruit
So various, not to taste that only tree
Of knowledge   *   *   *   *
——————— Then let us not think hard
One easy prohibition, who enjoy
The leave so large to all things else, and choice
Unlimited of manyfold delights:
But let us ever praise him, and extol
His bounty, following our delightful task
To prune these growing plants, and tend these
' flowers."

In this lovely scene and fruitful garden
were our first parents placed, and herein
they dwelt together in social happiness,
beholding the goodness of the Lord their
God, who had created them, for their own
happiness and his glory ; and receiving his
blessing, dwelling, as it were in his presence,
in an earthly paradise, where all was happiness and joy ; where the rose and the
voilet, the woodbine and the myrtle, shed
their fragrance around and where :—

"Each beauteous flower,
Iris all hues, roses, and jessamine,

Rear'd high their flourish'd heads between and
   wrought
Mosaic; under foot the violet,
Crocus, and hyacinth; with rich inlay,
Broider'd the ground, more colour'd than with stores
Of costliest emblem :"
Milton, Par. Lost.

Where the laurel and ivy, the box and the holly, displayed their luxurient greenness and beauty; and the vine and fig trees bended with timely fruit, intermixed with a number of other—

  "Goodliest trees, loaden with fairest fruit,
Blossoms, and fruits, at once of golden hue,
Appear'd with gay enamell'd colours mix'd."

And where also the wolf and the lamb; the leopard and the kid gambolled and played together; and the lion and ox fed together, and—

  "About them frisking play'd
All beasts of the earth, since wild, and of all chase
In wood or wilderness, forest or den;
Sporting the lion romp'd, and in his paw

Dandled the kid ; bears, tigers, ounces, pards
Gambol'd before them ; th' unwieldy elephant
To make them mirth, us'd all his might."

Milton, Par. Lost.

In this delightful and holy place dwelt
our first parents in virtuous simplicity and
spotless innocence.

CHAPTER III.

Little did our guileless progenitors, in
this happy state, imagine that any one was
plotting, if possible, their ruin, but truly
such was the case.   The devil, that arch-
enemy of happiness, virtue, and innocence
was using all his hellish wit and spite to

urge them if possible by false deceit to
break the commands of their Creator

> " For now
> Satan, now first inflamed with rage, came down
> The tempter, ere th' accuser of mankind,
> To wreak on innocent, frail man his loss
> Of that first battle, and his flight to hell."

Little also did our first happy parents
imagine that they should, by one unguard-
ed moment, partake of the forbidden fruit,
and thereby bring death, sin, and all their
train of evils upon themselves and their
offsprings. But, alas, such was to be the
case, for Satan, with all his hellish malice,
joined by all his devilish crew, were endea-
vouring with all their might and main to
cause their fall; and for their certain
accomplishment of it they, no doubt, selec-
ted the serpent as the most likely animal
to affect their evil design, as being the
most wise, cunning, and subtle of all the
beasts of the earth; for Christ, in his

charge to his disciples, commands them to be as wise as serpents and harmless as doves.*

But here the Athiest, the Deist and the, Infidel may raise a demur, and say it is all nonsence and ridiculous to assert that a serpent tempted our first parents to sin, as being impossible for a serpent to speak, and that no one was ever heard to speak, and that, therefore, it was impossible for the innocent reptile to do such an act.

The reply that is here needful is very short, for all Christians will truly believe, with myself, that the devil like themselves but a little more artful than them, because he is their leader, can manage to eke out of a very lame case an excellent, but blind substitute, or argument to further his ends; for Satan himself is transformed into an angel of light,† and no marvel that he, therefore, should transform or enter him-

---

* Matt. x. 16.   † 2 Cor. xi. 14.

self into the serpent, for the surer accomplishment of his diabolical design.

Now the serpent was more subtle than any beast of the field which the Lord God had made. And he said unto the woman, " Yea, hath God said, ye shall not eat of every tree of the garden.

——— " Close the serpent sly,
Insinuating, wove with Gordian twine,
His braided twine, and of his fatal guile
Gave proof."———

The woman said of every tree of the garden we may freely eat, except the tree in the midst of the garden, which our Maker hath commanded us not to eat, neither shall ye touch it lest ye die. For in the day that thou eatest thereof thou shalt surely die.*

"Ah gentle pair, ye little think how nigh
Your change approaches, when all these delights
Will vanish, and deliver you to woe;
More woe. the more your taste is now of joy."

Gen. ii. 17.

No, no, said the serpent, you shall not surely die, for in the day that you eat thereof, your eyes will be opened, and you will be as God's, knowing good and evil; so the woman being enticed in this artful manner, by this subtle demon; and seeing that the fruit of the tree was good for food, pleasant to the eyes, and a tree to be desired; because she was told that it would make them more wise.* Therefore she ventured to pluck and eat, and also to give unto her husband of the fruit of the forbidden tree, and he did eat.

> "She gave him of that fair enticing fruit
> With liberal hand: he scrupled not to eat,
> Against his better knowledge; not deceived,
> But fondly overcome with female charms."

> "Earth felt the wound : and nature from her seat
> Sighing, through all her works, gave signs of woe,
> That all was lost."——

And now, alas, came that fatal knowledge which they desired, for the eyes of

* Gen. iii. 6.

both were opened; their virtue and innocence were gone; and they knew that they were naked, and they sewed fig leaves together and made themselves aprons to hide their shame, and to cover themselves that the shame of their nakedness need not appear.* For

————————Innocence, that as a veil
Had shadow'd them from knowing ill, was gone
Just confidence, and native righteousness,
And honour, from about them naked left
To guilty shame————

Bad fruit of knowledge if this be to know
Which leaves us naked thus, of honour void
Of innocence, of faith, of purity.
                    Milton, Par. Lost, Book 9.

For before they had broken the command of their Creator "They saw not that they were naked," for they looked not on themselves. They considered not themselves; obeyed not their own wills; and walked not in their own ways. Their eyes were

* Rev. iii. 18.

fixed on God: their wills were bound up in his. And it was only when, in tasting of the forbidden tree, they looked as it were away from Him, that "The eyes of them both were opened, and they knew that they were naked," that they felt in shame the first sad consequence of sin.

CHAPTER IV.

"Sin-stricken world!
Why are there clouds to gall thine open brow.
Ah! when the miser doats o'er muir and glen,
Why doth heart-sickness mar his pleasures glow,
And pine in thoughts beyond a strangers ken?
Sin hath been here—hath furrow'd o'er the sod,
And claims an orphaned earth—an earth without
a God.
Sin-stricken world."
                    The Churchman's Mon. Pen. Mag.

Man has therefore broken the commands of his Maker, and thereby fallen from his high state of innocence and happiness, and is become a sinner. Death and sin hath entered into the world, and man's condition now is mortal as to his body, and sinful as to his soul. But he is not left in his fallen and lost state without hope, for after Adam and Eve had partaken of the forbidden tree, they heard, as usual, the voice of the

Lord God walking in the garden, in the
cool of the day,* but, alas, not with that
degree of confidence and pleasure as they
was wont, for they were afraid of his glorious presence and hid themselves amongst
the trees of the garden to avoid, if possible,
being seen by him, for they were ashamed
and afraid to appear before him.

But the Lord God called unto Adam,
and said unto him, Where art thou.*
Therefore Adam knowing that he was no
longer concealed, was forced to appear before his Maker, whose commands he had
broken, to answer for his ungrateful con-
duct.

" He came : and with him Eve, more loath, tho'
  first
To offend ; discountenanced both, and discomposed:
Love were not in their looks, either to God,
Or to each other ; but apparent guilt,
And shame, and perturbation, and despair."

Milton, Par. Lost.

* Gen. iii. 9.

And he said, 1 heard thy voice in the garden, and I was afraid, because I was naked.* Therefore we see a guilty conscience needs no accusing for it will accuse itself. And the Lord said unto him, who told thee that thou wast naked. Hast thou eaten of the forbidden fruit; and Adam, to screen himself, said, The woman, whom thou gavest to be with me, she gave me of the tree and I did eat. To whom the Lord said, Woman, what is this that thou hast done? And she, to clear herself, cast all the blame upon the serpent; saying, The serpent beguiled me and I did eat. Which when the Lord God heard, without delay, he proceeded to judgment on the accused serpent.

> " Yet God at last
> To Satan, first in sin, his doom applied,
> Though in mysterious times, judged as then best,
> And on the serpent thus his curse let fall."

Because thou hast done this, thou art cur-

Ibib. iii. 10.

sed above all cattle, and above every beast
of the field: upon thy belly shalt thou go,
and dust shalt thou eat all the days of thy
life. And I will put enmity between thee
and the woman, and between thy seed and
her seed it shall bruise thy head, and thou
shalt bruise his heel. Which was truly
accomplished by the Son of God, who was
born of the Virgin Mary, when he died
upon the cross, and arose from the grave
the third day ; (for truly thereby he bruised
Satan's kingdom, who was the head or stig-
nator of the serpent when he tempted our
first parents to pluck and eat the forbidden
fruit) for when he ascended up on high, he
led captivity captive and gave gifts unto
men.* And unto the woman he said, I
will greatly multiply thy sorrow, and thy
conception, in sorrow thou shalt bring forth
children.

And unto Adam, he said, Because thou

* Eph. iv. 8.

hast harkened unto the voice of thy wife,
and not unto my commands, and hast partaken of the tree which I commanded thee
not to touch, cursed is the ground for thy
sake. In sorrow, (that is by servile labour)
shalt thou eat of it all the days of thy life.
Thorns also, and thistles, and weeds shall
it bring forth, and thou shalt eat the herb
of the field; * and for thy disobedience
thou shalt till the ground; and the bread
that thou eatest shall only be procured by
the sweat of thy brow, till thou return to
the earth, out of it thou was taken, for
dust thou art, and unto dust thou shalt
return.

So did their Maker pass judgment upon
them. But divine justice was mingled
with mercy, for their offended Father beheld them with compassion.

> " Then pitying how they stood
> Before him naked to the air, that now
> Must suffer change,————

Gen. iii. 16—18.

As Father of his family he clad
Their nakedness with skins of beasts."

Therefore the Lord God sent them forth
from the garden of Eden to till the ground
from which they were taken, having only
enjoyed their happy state of holiness, innocence, and virtue, for the short space of a
few months ; for by their disobedience they
forfeited their joy and happiness, and

" Brought death into the world, and all our woe
With loss of Eden."

So he drove out the man ; and he placed
at the east of the garden of Eden, Cherubims and a flaming sword which turned
every way, to keep the way of the tree of
life.*

Gen. iii. 24.

CHAPTER V.

"But well thou know'st
Our God hath mingled, in his awful curse,
Mercies, with threatenings In these mystic words
Thy seed shall bruise the serpent's head 'tis hid;
We may not fathom the mysterious depth
Where rest th' Omnipotent's decrees—but yet
That promise wisper'd hope, triumphant joy,
Victorious conquest over sin and death !

Mary Ann Cursham.

Adam and Eve were now expelled from
their lovely and delightful situation,—the
beautiful garden of Eden,—into an uncul-
tivated and dreary world ; and to prevent
their return into the garden of Eden, the
Lord God placed at the entrance cherubims
and a flaming sword. They were, therefore, now in a wilderness of thorns and
briers, thistles and weeds ; infested with
wild birds and beasts of prey, devouring

each other, and growling revenge upon
each other. Birds and beasts, which before the disobedience of man, were tame
and lovely to each other, but which,
through his fall, were rendered wild, fierce,
and savage. In this dreary wilderness,
were our first parents placed after their
transgression to erect themselves an habi-
tation, and to till the hard and crusty
ground, for to grow corn and herbs for their
food and sustenance. But blessed be Almighty God he left them not in this dreary
and waste wilderness (although they had
so abused his kindness and goodness) without an encouraging glance and ray of hope.
For although the ground was cursed for
their sakes, yet the time was to come,
when instead of the thorn, shall come up
the fir tree, and instead of the brier shall
come up the myrtle tree, and it shall be to
the Lord for a name, for an everlasting
sign that shall not be cut off,* and through

* Isai. lv. 13.

their fall, the beasts of the field were rendered wild, savage, and enemies to each other. Yet the time was to come when The wolf also shall dwell with the lamb, and the leopard shall lie down with the kid ; and the calf and the young lion and the fatling together, and a little child shall lead them. And the cow and the bear shall feed ; their young ones shall lie down together ; and the lion shall eat straw like the ox ; and the suckling child shall play on the hole of the asp, and the weaned child shall put his hand on the cockatrice's den. They shall not hurt nor destroy in all my holy mountain, for the earth shall be full of the knowledge of the Lord, as the waters cover the sea * Thus was the seed of the woman to bruise the serpent's head. But four thousand years was to roll along and pass away before the glorious and auspicious event was accomplished, and patriarchs, prophets, and priests were

*Isa.xi. 6—8.

to prophecy and foretell of the coming of
him who was to bruise the serpent's head ;
and typical designs and shadows of the law,
were to pourtray the glory and excellency
of him who was to come and offer himself
as the One great sacrifice for the redemption of fallen man, and who was to be the
true Light which was to lighten every one
that cometh into the world.* And in due
time this glorious light was made manifest
to take away the sins of the world, herald-
ded in by his messenger John the Baptist,
who was sent to prepare the way of the
Lord ; and which is described by the prophets Isaiah and Malachi so accurately as
if they had been upon the earth when the
herald of the Highest proclaimed to the
world that the King of kings, and Lord of
lords was a sojourner upon this lower earth.
In these words, Behold the Lamb of God
which taketh away the sin of the world.†
So now the book of prophecy is sealed.

* St. John ii. 9.　　† St. John i. 29.

The types and shadows of the Jewish sac-
rifices are now brought to light by the appearance of him who is to bruise (the kingdom of Satan) the head of the serpent.

" Israel in ancient days
Not only had a view
Of Sinai in a blaze,
But learn'd the gospel too.
The types and figures were a glass
In which they saw a Saviour's face.

The paschal sacrifice,
And blood-besprinkled door,
Seen with enlightened eyes,
And once applied with power.
Would teach the need of other blood
To reconcile the world to God.

The lamb, the dove set forth
His perfect innocence,
Whose blood of matchless worth
Should be the soul's defence.
For he who can for sin atone
Must have no failings of his own.

The scape-goat on his head
The people's trespass bore,
And to the desert led
Was to be seen no more.

In him our Surety seem'd to say,
Behold, I bear your sins away.

Dipt in his fellow's blood,
The living bird went free,
The type well understood,
Express'd the sinner's plea.
Describ'd a guilty soul enlarg'd,
And by a Saviour's death discharg'd.

Jesus, I love to trace
Throughout the sacred page,
The footsteps of thy grace,
The same in every age.
O grant that I may faithful be,
To clearer light vouchsaf'd to me."

CHAPTER VI.

Beautiful world !
"For thou art beautiful, ev'n in decay,
Fair in thy tears—bright in thy funeral weeds ;
The whole creation groaneth till the day
Of holy ransom shall confirm the deeds
Of Calvary's sufferer ; when th' adopted race
Shall close in glory, the domain of grace,
When 'mid the garden trees at eve of day,
The voice Almighty shall be heard in love,
And man shall joy to wend his happy way
Through smiling Eden's consecrated grove.
Beautiful world !"

F. J.

Behold, the time is now arrived for the
redemption of fallen man, and Christ, the
true Messiah, appears on earth for the
accomplishment of the stupendous work ;
but not in that regal splendour and glory
as the Jews expected him to appear in, for
they looked to have beheld him to appear

and to reign as an earthly king in pomp
and state, and to have delivered them from
their earthly enemies; but such was not
the case; his was far a more important
office, namely, to deliver us from the pow-
ers of darkness, and to redeem us from the
curse of a broken law.* And for that purpose he made himself of no reputation,
but took upon him the form of a servant.
Was made in the likeness of men, and was
born a babe in Bethlehem. And instead
of his birth being made known, and honored
by the rich, the noble, and the great, it
was made known unto a few poor shepherds who were keeping watch over their
flocks by night, by an angel who appeared
unto them, and which said unto them, fear
not, for behold I bring you good tidings of
great joy, which shall be to all people. For
unto you is born this day, in the city of
David, a Saviour, which is Christ the

* Gal. iii. 13.

D

Lord; (which was no doubt done to repre-
sent to the world, that Christ the true
Messiah, was come into the world to be
the Saviour and Shepherd of fallen man;
and which is so beautifully described and
foretold by the prophet Isaiah in these
words,—He shall feed his flock like a
shepherd: he shall gather the lambs with
his arm, and carry them in his bosom, and
shall gently lead those that are with young*)
And Christ himself says, I am the good
Shepherd, and know my sheep, and am
known of mine.†

After they had seen the angel of the
Lord, they went with haste to Bethlehem,
and found Mary and Joseph, and the babe
divine, lying in a manger; and when the
time was accomplished for the circumcise-
ing of the child his name was called Jesus,
which was so named of the angel before he
was conceived in the womb. And the

*Isa. xl. 11.　　†St John x. 14.

child Jesus grew, and waxed strong in spirit, filled with wisdom and the grace of God was upon him ; and at twelve years of age he was found by his parents, who had lost him, sitting among the doctors of the law, both hearing and asking them questions, in the temple. And when he was thirty years of age he was baptized by John in the river Jordan, and there the Holy Spirit descended upon him like a dove, accompanied with a voice from heaven, which said, This is my beloved Son in whom I am well pleased.*

After he had been baptized he was led by the Spirit into the wilderness, and there he was tempted by the devil forty days and forty nights. † And when his temptations where ended, he returned from the wilderness unto the Mount of Olives, and there delivered that excellent discourse, called " Christ's sermon in the Mount ; " he then

* Matt. iii. 17;   † Luke iv. 2.

went from village to village, and from town
to town; healing the sick, restoring the
blind their sight, unstopping the deaf ears,
and unloosing the tongues of those that
were dumb, and proclaiming to all around
the Gospel of Peace.

Such was the life of Christ—a life of
usefulness—a life of toil and sorrow—and
a life of care and pain; all of which he
endured for rebellious man, and which
shewed plainly that he was the Son of God,
which was to come into the world to be the
propitiation for our sins. And when the
time came when he was to accomplish the
grand design, and depart out of this world
unto his Father. He was betrayed into
the hands of the Chief Priests and Cap-
tains, who took him and crucified him
upon the cross between two thieves, where
he endured the sneers and scoffs of the
spectators, and the wrath of an offended
God; and so great was his sufferings that
the sun hid its glorious face and refused to

shine. The solid earth trembled from its
foundations, and all nature appeared confused. And Jesus cried with a loud voice,
and gave up the ghost; and the third day
he rose again from the dead, and appeared
to his disciples; and then ascended up into
heaven, where he now lives and intercedes
for sinners. So now man's redemption is
complete, for Jesus was born to die and
and rise again for the recovery of man
from his dreadful fall. And at the end of
the world this same Jesus will appear again
to judge the world, but not in that low
estate in which he appeared to redeem the
world, for he will come attended with angels and archangels, and all the host of
heaven: for the Lord himself shall descend
from heaven with a shout, with the voice
of the archangel, and the trumpet of God.*
And then shall the heavens pass away with
a great noise, and the elements shall melt
with fervent heat; the earth also, and all

* Thess. iv. 16.

the works that are therein shall be burned up. But before that great and notable day, the Gospel must be preached in all the nations under heaven,* which was commenced by the apostles of Jesus Christ at the command of their Master, who said unto them Go ye into all the world, and preach the Gospel to every creature; and which is carried on by each successive minister of each denomination of Christians; and which shall be till the earth be filled with the knowledge of the Lord, and then shall each nation beat their swords into ploughshares, and their spears into pruning hooks. Nation shall not lift up a sword against nation; neither shall they learn war any more,† for brotherly love shall link each other together in friendship and harmony; and the time is not far distant when these things shall be accomplished— for besides the infallible word of God, the signs of the times, and the various means

* Matt. xxiv. 14.   † Micah iv. 3.

which Providence has brought into operation within the last fifty years, especially
indicate the approaching accomplishment
of all the merciful purposes of God towards
mankind. Scriptural truth appears to be
better understood by the Church of God,
and a spirit of candour and love prevails in
it, in such a degree as never characterized
it since the Apostolic age. Christians of
different denominations, manifest a greater disposition to merge their peculiarities,
uniting in the grand essentials of evangeli-
cal religion, to extend the kingdom of their
Saviour in blessing the whole family of
man. For this purpose Missionary Socie-
ties have been established upon a plan to
embrace the whole world. They are sup-
ported by the voluntary contributions of
the several bodies of Christians, whose
agents have been eminently honored of
God in diffusing the saving knowledge of
Jesus Christ.

By their means whole nations have aban-

doned idolatry with its degrading brutali-
ties, and multitudes of them have received
the truth as it is in Jesus. It is computed
that a thousand Protestant Missionaries are
disseminating the doctrines of their Saviour
among the Heathen, assisted by at least a
thousand preachers and' teachers from
among the native converts.

To further their objects, the Scriptures
have been translated by the missionaries
into about sixty different languages, which
before, had never been sanctified by the
inspired word of God; and the Bible So-
ciety has published the Scriptures in whole
or in part, in about one hundred and fifty
languages. Innumerable religious Tracts
have been published in various languages.
Schools have been established at the various Missionary stations; and it is calcula-
ted that not less than 100,000 Pagan children and adults are receiving Christian instruction in day and Sunday schools. The
cause of Jesus Christ in the evangelization

of the world is gaining an increase of
friends and supporters. The several go-
vernments are becoming more favourable
to Christian missions. The fruits of evan-
gelical instruction are appearing in multitudes of devoted converts to Christ among
the heathen; and the morning, we trust,
has evidently dawned upon the world which
shall be succeeded by the rising of the sun
of righteousness, and by the meridian glory
of truth and holiness, when all shall know
the Lord from the least even to the great-
est, and the kingdoms of this world shall
become the kingdoms of our God and of
his Christ.

And now, in conclusion, I would ask,
gentle reader, dost thou believe that this
Saviour is willing and able to cleanse and
purify thee from all thy sins; if thou dost,
happy is thy case. Only believe, and thou
shalt be saved; put thy trust in Him, and
he shall preserve and bring thee unto life
eternal. But if on the contrary thou count

his blood as an unholy thing, and not in
any way applicable to the cleansing of thy
unholy and sinful soul; if thou slight his
offered grace, and still continue to do, dis-
pite to his goodness, then horrible is thy
situation, for remember, the Lord Jesus
shall be revealed from heaven, with his
mighty angels in flaming fire, taking vengeance on them that know not God, and
obey not the Gospel of our Lord Jesus
Christ, who shall be punished with everlasting destruction from the presence of
the Lord, and from the glory of his power.*
Oh, therefore, remain no longer a stranger
to Him and to His saving grace, but turn
to him with your whole heart. Confess
your sins ; trust to his merits for pardon
and acceptance, through his blood and then
he will become your friend, yea, your Saviour, and the God of your salvation.

And to you who have come to him for
salvation, as poor, blind, naked, and miser-

* 2 Thess. i. 7—9.

able sinners, who have believed the promises and have got pardon and peace through believing, and in whose hearts dwells the Holy Ghost, the Divine Comforter. Go on in your most holy faith; rely wholly on Him, and He shall sustain you and bring your souls to the desired haven at last.

Now the God of peace that brought again from the dead our Lord Jesus, that great Shepherd of the sheep, through the blood of the everlasting covenant. Make us perfect in every good work to do his will, working in us that which is well-pleasing in his sight, through Jesus Christ, to whom be glory for ever and ever. Amen.

————————Moriri

Non. sibi. sed illi populi.

He comes: he comes the Saviour of mankind;
The true Messiah; by ancient prophets, foretold.
God's eternal Son on earth appears—
In mortal flesh. A babe in Bethlehem,
The Prince of Peace.—Ruler of the world
Deigns to be born: for man's redemption,

In a stable; with only a manger for his cradle.
He grows up to manhood, and raises the dead;
Heals the sick, restores the blind their sight;
Loosens the stammering and dumb tongues;
Unstops the deaf ears, and feeds the hungry multi-
    tudes,
And for these kind acts, he his arrainged
Before the judgment seat of mortals,
And there condemned to die by sinful creatures.
Amazing love beyond description—
That the Son immortal should bear
The scoffs and insults of mere worms.
But view him bearing his own cross
Whereon he was to suffer, as a guilty malafactor.
No wrath nor vengeance mark'd his course,
But love through all his actions shone.
And when upon the cross he hung,
Between heaven and earth, in agonizing pain,
His voice was—" Father, forgive them,
" For they know not what they do."
Here was humility and love, which clearly spoke,
" This truly was the Son of God."—
He gives up the Ghost, his followers weep
To see their Lord and Leader so abus'd.
But tho' heaviness for a night endureth,
The morning light brings shining joy;
Their Master and guide no longer sleeps in death,
He's broke the barriers of the dreary grave,
And in full triumph rose therefrom.
In vain they tried to hold him there,

Altho' they watch'd and seal'd the stone,
Which to the door of the sepulchre, they'd roll'd,
For he's left the tomb and rose triumphant on high
Escorted there by heaven's most numerous host
Of shining angels, sent by his Father's command
To guard him to his throne above.
And now in heaven he lives and reigns,
And for sinners he continually intercedes.
The Father looks upon his Son, and smiles,
And then his dreadful vengeance ceaseth,
For the death of Christ is the golden key—
That unlocks again the gates of Paradise.
For now is sent the Gospel invitation,
And all may come and freely partake
Of the healing balm, "The Balm of Gilead!"

HYMN.

"OF A TRUTH THIS WAS THE SON OF GOD."

Centurion.

Well might the green clad mountains shake,
   The gorgeous temple rend in twain,
And the high and lofty rocks to quake
   When Jesus died to rise again.

Well might the sun refuse to shine
   And all his glories hide,
And earthquakes shake the solid ground.
   To humble mortals pride,

Well might the curtains of the night obscure
   The day, when creatures shed their Saviour's
      blood,
And the Centurion tremble, and be sure
   " This truly was the Son of God."

Well might angels veil their faces
   To see the King of glory thus abused
By worms of earth, whom he was come to save
   From ruin and an endless death.

HYMN.

O for a thousand tongues to sing
   My great Redeemer's praise,
The glories of my God and King,
   The triumphs of his grace.

Jesus, the name that charms our fears,
  That bids our sorrows cease ;
'Tis music in the sinner's ears,
  'Tis life, and health, and peace.

He breaks the power of cancell'd sin,
  He sets the prisoner's free ;
His blood can make the foulest clean,
  His blood avail'd for me.

He speaks, and listening to his voice,
  New life the dead receive ;
The mournful broken hearts rejoice,
  The humble poor believe.

Hear him, ye deaf ; his praise, ye dumb,
  Your loosen'd tongues employ ;
Ye blind, behold your Saviour comes,
  And leap, ye lame, for joy.

MATLOCK :

Printed by J. W. Adam, Museum Parade.

WORKS BY T. H. HOLMES.

THE CHRISTIAN'S CALL,

OR

NEW YEAR'S GIFT,

Price 2d.

Wherein the evil effects of "A party spirit" are pointed out,
and the injury they occasion to the cause of true religion.

Also, price 3d.,

A VISIT TO BUXTON,

In the High Peak of Derbyshire.

Giving a pleasing description of this ancient Wa-
tering Place, its Public Buildings, the beautiful
scenery that surrounds it, and also a short account
of the practice of Well Flowering, which is
annually performed there.

Printed and sold by G. Goodwin, Bakewell; also
by W. Saxton, High Street, Sheffield; J. W. Adam,
jun., Matlock Bath.